Plant-Based Sn Budget

Cheap and Tasty Plant-Based Snacks to Stay Fit and Save Money

Clay Palmer

Table of Contents

Queso Dip

Preparation time: 5 minutes Cooking time: 0 minute Servings: 6

Ingredients:

1 cup cashews ½ teaspoon minced garlic 1/2 teaspoon salt 1/2 teaspoon ground cumin 1 teaspoon red chili powder 2 tablespoons nutritional yeast 1 tablespoon harissa 1 cup hot water

Directions:

Place all the ingredients in a food processor and pulse for 2 minutes until smooth and well combined. Tip the dip in a bowl, taste to adjust seasoning and then serve.

Masala Popcorn

Preparation time: 5 minutes Cooking time: 15 minutes
Servings: 4

Ingredients:

3 cups popped popcorn 2 hot chili peppers, sliced 1 teaspoon ground cumin 6 curry leaves 1 teaspoon ground coriander 1/3 teaspoon salt 1/8 teaspoon chaat masala 1/4 teaspoon turmeric powder ¼ teaspoon red pepper flakes 1/4 teaspoon garam masala 1/3 cup olive oil

Directions:

Take a large pot, place it over medium heat, add half of the oil and when hot, add chili peppers and curry leaves and cook for 3 minutes until golden. When done, transfer curry leaves and pepper to a plate lined with paper towels and set aside until required. Add remaining oil into the pot, add remaining ingredients except for popcorns, stir until mixed and cook for 1 minute until fragrant. Then tip in popcorns, remove the pan from heat, stir well until coated, and then sprinkle with bay leaves and red chili. Toss until mixed and serve straight away.

Avocado Toast with Herbs and Peas

Preparation time: 10 minutes Cooking time: 0 minute

Servings: 4

Ingredients:

½ of a medium avocado, peeled, pitted, mashed 6 slices of radish 2 tablespoons baby peas ¼ teaspoon ground black pepper 1 teaspoon chopped basil ¼ teaspoon salt 1/2 lemon, juiced 1 slice of bread, whole-grain, toasted

Directions:

Spread mashed avocado on the one side of the toast and then top with peas, pressing them into the avocado. Layer the toast with radish slices, season with salt and black pepper, sprinkle with basil, and drizzle with lemon juice. Serve straight away.

Black Bean and Corn Quesadillas

Preparation time: 15 minutes Cooking time: 30 minutes Servings: 4

Ingredients:

For the Black Beans and Corn:

1/2 of a medium white onion, peeled, chopped 1/2 cup cooked black beans 1/2 cup cooked corn kernels 1 teaspoon minced garlic ½ of jalapeno, deseeded, diced 1/2 teaspoon salt 1 teaspoon red chili powder 1 teaspoon cumin 1 tablespoon olive oil

For the Quesadillas:

4 large corn tortillas 4 green onions, chopped ½ cup vegan nacho cheese sauce ½ cup chopped cilantro 1 large tomato, diced Salsa as needed for dipping

Directions:

Prepare beans and for this, take a frying pan, place it over medium-high heat, add oil and when hot, add onion, jalapeno, and garlic and cook for 3 minutes. Then add remaining ingredients, stir until mixed and cook for 2 minutes until hot. Take a large skillet pan, place over medium heat, place the tortilla in it and cook for 1 minute until toasted and then flip it. Spread some of the cheese sauce on one half of the top, spread with beans mixture, top with cilantro, onion, and tomato and then fold the filling with the other side of the tortilla. Pat down the tortilla, cook it for 2 minutes, then carefully flip it, continue cooking for 2 minutes until hot, and then slide to a plate. Cook remaining quesadilla in the same manner, then cut them into wedges and serve

Potato Chips

Preparation time: 10 minutes Cooking time: 20 minutes Servings: 2

Ingredients:

3 medium potatoes, scrubbed, thinly sliced, soaked in warm water for 10 min ½ teaspoon garlic powder ½ teaspoon onion powder ½ teaspoon red chili powder ½ teaspoon curry powder 1 teaspoon of sea salt 1 tablespoon apple cider vinegar 2 tablespoons olive oil

Directions:

Drain the potato slices, pat dry, then place them in a large bowl, add remaining ingredients and toss until well coated. Spread the potatoes in a single layer on a baking sheet and bake for 20 minutes until crispy, turning halfway. Serve straight away

Chocolate-Covered Almonds

Preparation time: 1 hour and 45 minutes Cooking time: 30 seconds Servings: 4

Ingredients:

8 ounces almonds 1/2 teaspoon sea salt 6 ounces chocolate disks, semisweet, melted

Directions:

Microwave chocolate in a heatproof bowl for 30 seconds until it melts, then dip almonds in it, four at a time, and place them on a baking sheet. Let almonds stand for 1 hour until hardened, then sprinkle with salt, and cool them in the refrigerator for 30 minutes. Serve straight away

Loaded Baked Potatoes

Preparation time: 10 minutes Cooking time: 32 minutes
Servings: 2

Ingredients:

1/2 cup cooked chickpeas 2 medium potatoes, scrubbed
1 cup broccoli florets, steamed 1/4 cup vegan bacon bits
2 tablespoons all-purpose seasoning ¼ cup vegan cheese
sauce 1/2 cup vegan sour cream

Directions:

Pierce hole in the potatoes, microwave them for 12
minutes over high heat setting until soft to touch, and
then bake them for 20 minutes at 450 degrees F until
very tender. Open the potatoes, mash the flesh with a
fork, then top evenly with remaining ingredients and
serve.

Zucchini and Amaranth Patties

Preparation time: 10 minutes Cooking time: 30 minutes Servings: 14

Ingredients:

1 1/2 cups shredded zucchini ½ of a medium onion, shredded 1 1/2 cups cooked white beans 1/2 cup amaranth seeds 1 teaspoon red chili powder 1/2 teaspoon cumin 1/2 cup cornmeal 1/4 cup flax meal 1 tablespoon salsa 1 1/2 cups vegetable broth

Directions:

Stir together stock and amaranth on a pot, bring it to a boil over medium-high heat, then switch heat to medium-low level and simmer until all the liquid is absorbed. Mash the white beans in a bowl, add remaining ingredients including cooked amaranth and stir until well mixed. Shape the mixture into patties, then place them on a baking sheet lined with parchment sheet and bake for 30 minutes until browned and crispy, turning halfway. Serve straight away.

Quinoa and Black Bean Burgers

Preparation time: 10 minutes Cooking time: 6 minutes Servings: 5

Ingredients:

1/4 cup quinoa, cooked 15 ounces cooked black beans 2 tablespoons minced white onion 1/4 cup minced bell pepper ½ teaspoon minced garlic 1/2 teaspoon salt 1 1/2 teaspoons ground cumin 1/2 cup bread crumbs 1 teaspoon hot pepper sauce 3 tablespoons olive oil 1 flax egg

Directions:

Place all the ingredients in a bowl, except for oil, stir until well combined, and then shape the mixture into five patties. Heat oil in a frying pan over medium heat, add patties and cook for 3 minutes per side until browned. Serve straight away.

Carrot Cake Bites

Preparation time: 15 minutes Cooking time: 0 minute Servings: 15

Ingredients:

2 cups oats, old-fashioned ½ cup grated carrot 2 cups coconut flakes, unsweetened 1/2 teaspoon salt 1 teaspoon cinnamon 1/2 cup maple syrup 1/2 teaspoon vanilla extract, unsweetened 1/2 cup almond butter 2 tablespoons white chocolate chips

Directions:

Place oats in a food processor, add coconut and pulse until ground. Then add remaining ingredients except for chocolate chips and pulse for 3 minutes until a sticky dough comes together. Add chocolate chips, pulse for 1 minute until just mixed, and then shape the mixture into fifteen small balls. Refrigerate the balls for 30 minutes and then serve

Kale Hummus

Preparation time: 5 minutes Cooking time: 0 minute Servings: 4

Ingredients:

2 cups cooked chickpeas 5 cloves of garlic, peeled 4 cups kale, torn into pieces 1 teaspoon of sea salt 1/3 cup lemon juice 1/4 cup olive oil 1/4 cup tahini

Directions:

Place all the ingredients in a bowl and pulse for 2 minutes until smooth. Tip the hummus in a bowl, drizzle with oil, and then serve.

Rice Pizza

Preparation time: 10 minutes Cooking time: 35 minutes Servings: 6

Ingredients:

For the Crust: 1 1/2 cup short-grain rice, cooked 1/2 teaspoon garlic powder 1 teaspoon coconut sugar 1 tablespoon red chili flakes

For the Sauce: 1/4 teaspoon onion powder 1 tablespoon nutritional yeast 1/4 teaspoon garlic powder 1/4 teaspoon ginger powder 1 tablespoon red chili flakes 1 teaspoon soy sauce 1/2 cup tomato purée

For the Toppings: 2 1/2 cups oyster mushrooms 1 chili pepper, deseeded, sliced 2 scallions, sliced 1 teaspoon coconut sugar 1 teaspoon soy sauce Baby corn as needed

Directions:

Prepare the crust and for this, place all of its ingredients in a bowl and stir until well combined. Then take a pizza pan, line it with parchment sheet, place rice mixture in it, spread it evenly, and then bake for 20 minutes at 350 degrees F. Then spread tomato sauce over the crust, top evenly with remaining ingredients for the topping and continue baking for 15 minutes. When done, slice the pizza into wedges and serve.

Jalapeno and Cilantro Hummus

Preparation time: 5 minutes Cooking time: 0 minute Servings: 4

Ingredients:

½ cup cilantro 1 1/2 cups chickpeas, cooked 1/2 of jalapeno pepper, sliced ½ teaspoon salt ½ teaspoon minced garlic 1 tablespoon lime juice 1/4 cup tahini ¼ water

Directions: Place all the ingredients in a bowl and pulse for 2 minutes until smooth. Tip the hummus in a bowl, drizzle with oil sprinkle with cilantro, and then serve.

Cinnamon Bun Balls

Preparation time: 15 minutes Cooking time: 0 minute Servings: 10

Ingredients:

5 Medjool dates, pitted 1/2 cup whole walnuts 1 tablespoon chopped walnuts 3 tablespoons ground cinnamon 1 teaspoon ground cardamom

Directions:

Place all the ingredients in a food processor, except for 1 tablespoon walnuts, and then process until smooth. Shape the mixture into ten balls, then roll them into chopped walnuts and serve

Nori Snack Rolls

Preparation Time: 5 minutes cooking time: 10 minutes serves: 4 rolls

Ingredients

2 tablespoons almond, cashew, peanut, or other nut butter 2 tablespoons tamari, or soy sauce 4 standard nori sheets 1 mushroom, sliced 1 tablespoon pickled ginger ½ cup grated carrots

Directions

Preparing the Ingredients. Preheat the oven to 350°F. Mix together the nut butter and tamari until smooth and very thick. Lay out a nori sheet, rough side up, the long way. Spread a thin line of the tamari mixture on the far end of the nori sheet, from side to side. Lay the mushroom slices, ginger, and carrots in a line at the other end (the end closest to you). Fold the vegetables inside the nori, rolling toward the tahini mixture, which will seal the roll. Repeat to make 4 rolls. Put on a baking sheet and bake for 8 to 10 minutes, or until the rolls are slightly browned and crispy at the ends. Let the rolls cool for a few minutes, then slice each roll into 3 smaller pieces.

Jicama and Guacamole

Preparation Time: 15 minutes cooking time: 0 minutes serves: 4

Ingredients

juice of 1 lime, or 1 tablespoon prepared lime juice 2 hass avocados, peeled, pits removed, and cut into cubes ½ teaspoon sea salt ½ red onion, minced 1 garlic clove, minced ¼ cup chopped cilantro (optional) 1 jicama bulb, peeled and cut into matchsticks

Directions

Preparing the Ingredients. In a medium bowl, squeeze the lime juice over the top of the avocado and sprinkle with salt. Lightly mash the avocado with a fork. Stir in the onion, garlic, and cilantro, if using. Serve with slices of jicama to dip in guacamole. To store, place plastic wrap over the bowl of guacamole and refrigerate. The guacamole will keep for about 2 days.

Hot Avocado Bites

Preparation time: 5 minutes Cooking time: 15 minutes Servings: 4

Ingredients:

2 avocados, peeled, pitted and roughly cubed 2 tablespoons avocado oil 2 teaspoon chili powder 1 teaspoon sweet paprika 1 teaspoon rosemary, dried

Directions:

In a b owl, combine the avocados with the oil and the other ingredients, toss, spread them on a baking sheet lined with parchment paper and cook at 400 degrees F for 15 minutes. Divide the avocado bites into bowls and serve as a snack.

Lemony-Avocado Cilantro Shake

Preparation time: 5 minutes Cooking time: 0 minutes Servings: 1

Ingredients:

½ cup half and half 1 packet Stevia, or more to taste ¼ avocado, meat scooped 1 tbsp chopped cilantro 3 tbsps coconut oil What you'll need from the store cupboard: 1 ½ cups water

Directions

Add all ingredients in a blender. Blend until smooth and creamy. Serve and enjoy.

Coconut-Melon Yogurt Shake

Preparation time: 5 minutes Cooking time: 0 minutes Servings: 1

Ingredients:

¼ cup half and half 3 tbsp coconut oil ½ cup melon, slices 1 tbsp coconut flakes, unsweetened 1 tbsp chia seeds What you'll need from the store cupboard: 1 ½ cups water 1 packet Stevia, or more to taste

Directions

Add all ingredients in a blender. Blend until smooth and creamy. Serve and enjoy.

Lettuce Green Shake

Preparation time: 5 minutes Cooking time: 0 minutes Servings: 1

Ingredients:

¾ cup whole milk yogurt 2 cups 5-lettuce mix salad greens 3 tbsp MCT oil 1 tbsp chia seeds What you'll need from the store cupboard: 1 ½ cups water 1 packet Stevia, or more to taste

Directions

Add all ingredients in a blender. Blend until smooth and creamy. Serve and enjoy.

Butternut Squash Fries

Preparation time: 5 minutesCooking time: 40 minutes Servings: 2

Ingredients:

Ketchup for serving Kosher salt ½ butternut squash Cooking spray

Directions:

Set the oven at 425 degrees. Peel and remove the seeds of the butternut squash. Slice it in half. Cut it into fries. Cover a baking sheet with parchment paper and coat it with cooking spray. Sprinkle it with some salt. Place the fries into the baking sheet and bake for 40 minutes and flip it once. The fries are done once it begins to turn golden brown on the edges. Serve with the syrup if desired.

Olive Pimiento Quiche

Preparation time: 5 minutesCooking time: 50 minutes
Servings: 2

Ingredients:

1 Short-Crust Pastry 2 eggs ½ lb. Swiss cheese, coarsely grated 1 large onion, peeled, halved, and sliced 2 cloves garlic, peeled and thinly sliced 2 Tbs. olive oil ¼ cup sliced, cured Greek olives (black) 1 cup cream ½ cup sliced (roasted and peeled) pimiento pepper salt pepper to taste

Directions:

Prepare the short crust, line an 11-inch quiche pan with it, and prebake according to Directions. Sauté the sliced onions and garlic in the olive oil until they are golden brown. Distribute them evenly over the bottom of the pastry shell. Spread the grated cheese over the onions and garlic. Beat the eggs and cream together with a little salt and pepper and pour them over the cheese. Arrange the sliced pimientos and olives on top of the cheese in an attractive pattern and bake the quiche for 15 minutes in a preheated oven at 450 degrees, then reduce the heat to 350 and bake for another 10 to 15 minutes, or until the top of the quiche is lightly browned in spots. The quiche may be served hot, but I think it's better if it is allowed to cool to room temperature or chilled before serving.

Parmesan Crepes

Preparation time: 5 minutesCooking time: 30 minutes
Servings: 2

Ingredients:

6 eggs, beaten 3 cups milk 1 cup flour 1 tsp. salt 3 Tbs. butter, melted ½ cup finely grated Parmesan cheese (real, well-aged, imported Parmesan) Olive oil

Directions:

Sift the flour and salt into a bowl and stir in the beaten eggs. Add the milk slowly, beating with a whisk, then beat in the melted butter and the grated Parmesan. The batter should be smooth and have the consistency of thick cream. Let the batter stand for an hour or two before making the crêpes. Heat your crêpe pan and melt about 2 teaspoons butter in it. When the butter is melted and the foam has subsided, pour in about 3 tablespoons of the batter and swirl it around to the edges of the pan immediately. The crepe should cook about a minute or so on each side. Add a bit of butter to the pan between crêpes to avoid sticking. Stack the crêpes on a plate as you make them. The crepes can be kept warm in the oven until all of them are done if you intend to eat them right away. Or they can be reheated like any other crêpes, wrapped tightly in foil, and put in a moderate oven for about 10 minutes. Furthermore, they can be wrapped around asparagus, spread with feta cheese filling and folded up, rolled around a stuffing of hearts of artichoke and palm, or of creamed mushrooms, and they can be used in constructing a savory crepe cake, to be cut in wedges.

Wild Mushroom Crepe

Preparation time: 5 minutesCooking time: 40 minutes
Servings: 2

Ingredients:

4 oz. dried black mushrooms ¾ lb. Gruyère cheese, grated tomato-pepper sauce 1½ Tbs. olive oil 4 cloves garlic, minced 3 Tbs. butter 1 large yellow onion, chopped ¼ cup red wine 2 large heads butter lettuce 2½ cups Béchamel Sauce 1 recipe Parmesan Crêpes 3 cups fresh tomato purée ⅔ cup finely chopped roasted pimiento 2 bay leaves 2 to 3 Tbs. red wine salt pepper Garnish paprika

Directions:

Put the dried mushrooms in a large bowl and cover them completely with hot water. Let them soak while you prepare the tomato sauce. Heat the olive oil in a large skillet and sauté the garlic in it until it is golden. Add the tomato purée, chopped pimiento, bay leaves, and wine, as well as salt and pepper to taste. Simmer the sauce gently for an hour or two, until it is reduced by half and quite thick. Allow the sauce to cool slightly. When the mushrooms have soaked for about ½ hour, take them, one by one, from the bowl and wash them each with great care to get rid of all the sand and grit. Strain the water in which they were soaked through muslin or through a coffee filter. Put the mushrooms through a food mill, using the fine blade, or else mince them finely with a knife. Melt the butter in a large skillet and sauté the onions for a few minutes. Then add the ground mushrooms, a little red wine, some salt and pepper to taste, and at least 2½ cups of the strained mushroom water. Let this mixture simmer gently, stirring it occasionally, until most of the liquid has been absorbed and it has the consistency of a thick mush. Blanch the lettuce in a large kettle of boiling water, leaving them in for several minutes. When they are quite wilted, remove the heads, drain them thoroughly, squeezing out all the water, and chop the lettuce. Mix the chopped lettuce with a few spoonful of the Béchamel Sauce (just enough to bind it) and salt to taste. Put a crepe in the center of an ovenproof serving platter or a shallow baking dish. Spread it with a thin layer of the mushroom mixture, extending it evenly to the edges. Place another crepe over this and spread it evenly with a thin layer of the tomato sauce. Put down another crêpe, a layer of the chopped lettuce, another crêpe, and an even, thin layer of grated cheese. Repeat this order twice more, just as if making a layer cake. Pour a little Béchamel over the cheese on the very top and sprinkle it lightly with paprika. Prepare the second crepe "cake" in the same manner, using the remaining mushroom filling, tomato sauce, and chopped lettuce. You should have about 1½ cups of Béchamel Sauce and a little grated cheese left over. Stir the cheese into the sauce. Bake crepe cake in a preheated 400-degree oven for about 20 minutes. Heat the remaining sauce. Serve the crêpe cake by cutting it in wedges and passing the sauce separately.

Hummus Quesadillas

Preparation time: 5 minutes Cooking time: 15 minutes
Servings: 1

Ingredients:

1 tortilla, whole wheat 1/4 cup diced roasted red peppers
1 cup baby spinach 1/3 teaspoon minced garlic ¼
teaspoon salt ¼ teaspoon ground black pepper 1/4
teaspoon olive oil 1/4 cup hummus Oil as needed

Directions:

Place a large pan over medium heat, add oil and when
hot, add red peppers and garlic, season with salt and
black pepper and cook for 3 minutes until sauté. Then
stir in spinach, cook for 1 minute, remove the pan from
heat and transfer the mixture in a bowl. Prepare
quesadilla and for this, spread hummus on one-half of
the tortilla, then spread spinach mixture on it, cover the
filling with the other half of the tortilla and cook in a pan
for 3 minutes per side until browned. When done, cut the
quesadilla into wedges and serve.

Avocado Tomato Bruschetta

Preparation time: 10 minutes Cooking time: 0 minute Servings: 4

Ingredients:

3 slices of whole-grain bread 6 chopped cherry tomatoes ½ of sliced avocado ½ teaspoon minced garlic ½ teaspoon ground black pepper 2 tablespoons chopped basil ½ teaspoon of sea salt 1 teaspoon balsamic vinegar

Directions:

Place tomatoes in a bowl, and then stir in vinegar until mixed. Top bread slices with avocado slices, then top evenly with tomato mixture, garlic and basil, and season with salt and black pepper. Serve straight

Salted Almonds

Preparation time: 5 minutes Cooking time: 20 minutes Servings: 4

Ingredients:

2 cups almonds 4 tablespoons salt 1 cup boiling water

Directions:

Stir the salt into the boiling water in a pan, then add almonds in it and let them soak for 20 minutes. Then drain the almonds, spread them in an even layer on a baking sheet lined with baking paper and sprinkle with salt. Roast the almonds for 20 minutes at 300 degrees F, then cool them for 10 minutes and serve.

Honey-Almond Popcorn

Preparation time: 5 minutes Cooking time: 10 minutes Servings: 4

Ingredients:

1/2 cup popcorn kernels 2 tablespoons honey 1/2 teaspoon sea salt 2 tablespoons coconut sugar 1 cup roasted almonds 1/4 cup walnut oil

Directions:

Take a pot, place it over medium-low heat, add oil and when it melts, add four kernels and wait until they sizzle. Then add remaining kernel, toss until coated, sprinkle with sugar, drizzle with honey, shut the pot with the lid, and shake the kernels until popped completely, adding almonds halfway. Once all the kernels have popped, season them with salt and serve straight away.

Watermelon Pizza

Preparation time: 10 minutes Cooking time: 0 minute Servings: 10

Ingredients:

1/2 cup strawberries, halved 1/2 cup blueberries 1 watermelon 1/2 cup raspberries 1 cup of coconut yogurt 1/2 cup pomegranate seeds 1/2 cup cherries Maple syrup as needed

Directions:

Cut watermelon into 3-inch thick slices, then spread yogurt on one side, leaving some space in the edges and then top evenly with fruits and drizzle with maple syrup. Cut the watermelon into wedges and then serve.

Rosemary Popcorn

Preparation time: 10 minutes Cooking time: 10 minutes
Servings: 4

Ingredients:

1/2 cup popcorn kernels 1/2 teaspoon sea salt 1 tablespoon and 1/2 teaspoon minced rosemary 3 tablespoons unsalted vegan butter 1/4 cup olive oil 1/3 teaspoon ground black pepper

Directions:

Take a pot, place it over medium-low heat, add oil and when it melts, add four kernels and wait until they sizzle. Then add remaining kernel, toss until coated, add 1 tablespoon minced rosemary, shut the pot with the lid, and shake the kernels until popped completely. Once all the kernels have popped, transfer them in a bowl, cook remaining rosemary into melted butter, then drizzle this mixture over popcorn and toss until well coated. Season popcorn with salt and black pepper, toss until mixed and serve.

Nooch Popcorn

Preparation time: 10 minutes Cooking time: 10 minutes Servings: 4

Ingredients:

1/3 cup nutritional yeast 1 teaspoon of sea salt 3 tablespoons coconut oil ½ cup popcorn kernels

Directions:

Place yeast in a large bowl, stir in salt, and set aside until required. Take a medium saucepan, place it over medium-high heat, add oil and when it melts, add four kernels and wait until they sizzle. Then add remaining kernel, toss until coated, shut the pan with the lid, and shake the kernels until popped completely. When done, transfer popcorns tot eh yeast mixture, shut with lid and shape well until coated. Serve straight away

Applesauce

Preparation time: 10 minutes Cooking time: 15 minutes Servings: 6

Ingredients:

4 pounds mixed apples, cored, ½-inch chopped 1 strip of orange peel, about 3-inch 1/2 cup coconut sugar 1/2 teaspoon salt 1 cinnamon stick, about 3-inch 2 tablespoons apple cider vinegar Apple cider as needed for consistency of the sauce

Directions:

Take a large pot, place apples in it, then add remaining ingredients except for cider, stir until mixed and cook for 15 minutes over medium heat until apples have wilted, stirring every 10 minutes. When done, remove the cinnamon stick and orange peel and puree the mixture by using an immersion blender until smooth and stir in apple cider until sauce reaches to desired consistency. Serve straight away.

Oven-Dried Grapes

Preparation time: 5 minutes Cooking time: 4 hours Servings: 4

Ingredients:

3 large bunches of grapes, seedless Olive oil as needed for greasing

Directions:

Spread grapes into two greased baking sheets and bake for 4 hours at 225 degrees F until semi-dried. When done, let the grape cool completely and then serve.

Zaatar Popcorn

Preparation time: 10 minutes Cooking time: 0 minute Servings: 8

Ingredients:

8 cups popped popcorns 1/4 cup za'atar spice blend ¾ teaspoon salt 4 tablespoons olive oil

Directions:

Place all the ingredients except for popcorns in a large bowl and whisk until combined. Then add popcorns, toss until well coated, and serve straight away.

Spinach and Artichoke Dip

Preparation time: 10 minutes Cooking time: 25 minutes Servings: 10

Ingredients:

28 ounces artichokes 1 small white onion, peeled, diced 1 1/2 cups cashews, soaked, drained 4 cups spinach 4 cloves of garlic, peeled 1 1 1/2 teaspoons salt 1/4 cup nutritional yeast 1 tablespoon olive oil 2 tablespoons lemon juice 1 1/2 cups coconut milk, unsweetened

Directions:

Cook onion and garlic in hot oil for 3 minutes until saute and then set aside until required. Place cashews in a food processor; add 1 teaspoon salt, yeast, milk, and lemon juice and pulse until smooth. Add spinach, onion mixture, and artichokes and pulse until the chunky mixture comes together. Tip the dip in a heatproof dish and bake for 20 minutes at 425 degrees F until the top is browned and dip bubbles. Serve straight away with vegetable sticks.

Beans and Spinach Tacos

Preparation time: 10 minutes Cooking time: 15 minutes Servings: 4

Ingredients:

12 ounces spinach 4 tablespoons cooked kidney beans ½ of medium red onion, peeled, chopped ½ teaspoon minced garlic 1 medium tomato, chopped 3 tablespoons chopped parsley ½ of avocado, sliced ½ teaspoon ground black pepper 1 teaspoon salt 2 tablespoons olive oil 4 slices of vegan brie cheese 4 tortillas, about 6-inches

Directions:

Take a skillet pan, place it over medium heat, add oil and when hot, add onion and cook for 10 minutes until softened. Then stir in spinach, cook for 4 minutes until its leaves wilts, then drain it and distribute evenly between tortillas. Top evenly with remaining ingredients, season with black pepper and salt, drizzle with lemon juice and then serve.

Beetroot Hummus

Preparation time: 10 minutes Cooking time: 60 minutes Servings: 4

Ingredients:

15 ounces cooked chickpeas 3 small beets 1 teaspoon minced garlic 1/2 teaspoon smoked paprika 1 teaspoon of sea salt 1/4 teaspoon red chili flakes 2 tablespoons olive oil 1 lemon, juiced 2 tablespoon tahini 1 tablespoon chopped almonds 1 tablespoon chopped cilantro

Directions:

Drizzle oil over beets, season with salt, then wrap beets in a foil and bake for 60 minutes at 425 degrees F until tender. When done, let beet cool for 10 minutes, then peel and dice them and place them in a food processor. Add remaining ingredients and pulse for 2 minutes until smooth, tip the hummus in a bowl, drizzle with some more oil, and then serve straight away.

Chipotle and Lime Tortilla Chips

Preparation time: 10 minutes Cooking time: 15 minutes Servings: 4

Ingredients:

12 ounces whole-wheat tortillas 4 tablespoons chipotle seasoning 1 tablespoon olive oil 4 limes, juiced

Directions:

Whisk together oil and lime juice, brush it well on tortillas, then sprinkle with chipotle seasoning and bake for 15 minutes at 350 degrees F until crispy, turning halfway. When done, let the tortilla cool for 10 minutes, then break it into chips and serve.

Buffalo Quinoa Bites

Preparation time: 15 minutes Cooking time: 30 minutes Servings: 20

Ingredients:

For the Bites: 1 cup cooked quinoa 15 ounces cooked white beans 3 tablespoons chickpea flour 1 medium shallot, peeled, chopped 3 cloves of garlic, peeled ½ teaspoon ground black pepper 1/2 teaspoon salt 1 teaspoon smoked paprika 1/4 cup vegan buffalo sauce

For the Dressing: 1/4 cup chives 2 tablespoons hemp hearts 1 tablespoon nutritional yeast 1 teaspoon garlic powder 1 teaspoon onion powder 1/2 teaspoon salt ½ teaspoon ground black pepper 2 teaspoons dried dill 1 lemon, juiced 1/4 cup tahini 3/4 cup water

Directions:

Prepare the bites, and for this, place half of the beans in a food processor, add garlic and shallots, and pulse for 2 minutes until mixture comes together. Then add all the spices of the bites and buffalo sauce and pulse for 2 minutes until smooth. Add remaining beans along with chickpea flour and quinoa and pulse until just combined. Tip the mixture in a dish, shape it in the dough, shape it into twenty balls, about the golf-ball size, and bake for

30 minutes at 350 degrees F until crispy and browned, turning halfway. Meanwhile, prepare the dressing and for this, place all of its ingredients in a food processor and pulse for 2 minutes until smooth. Serve bites with prepared dressing.

Avocado and Sprout Toast

Preparation time: 5 minutes Cooking time: 0 minute

Servings: 4

Ingredients:

1/2 of a medium avocado, sliced 1 slice of whole-grain bread, toasted 2 tablespoons sprouts 2 tablespoons hummus ¼ teaspoon lemon zest ½ teaspoon hemp seeds ¼ teaspoon red pepper flakes

Directions:

Spread hummus on one side of the toast and then top with avocado slices and sprouts. Sprinkle with lemon zest, hemp seeds, and red pepper flakes and then serve straight away.

Thai Snack Mix

Preparation time: 15 minutes Cooking time: 90 minutes
Servings: 4

Ingredients:

5 cups mixed nuts 1 cup chopped dried pineapple 1 cup
pumpkin seed 1 teaspoon onion powder 1 teaspoon garlic
powder 2 teaspoons paprika 1/2 teaspoon ground black
pepper 1 teaspoon of sea salt 1/4 cup coconut sugar 1/2
teaspoon red chili powder 1 tablespoon red pepper flakes
1/2 tablespoon red curry powder 2 tablespoons soy sauce
2 tablespoons coconut oil

Directions:

Switch on the slow cooker, add all the ingredients in it
except for dried pineapple and red pepper flakes, stir
until combined and cook for 90 minutes at high heat
setting, stirring every 30 minutes. When done, spread
the nut mixture on a baking sheet lined with parchment
paper and let it cool. Then spread dried pineapple on top,
sprinkle with red pepper flakes and serve.

Zucchini Chips

Preparation time: 10 minutes Cooking time: 120 minutes Servings: 4

Ingredients:

1 large zucchini, thinly sliced 1 teaspoon salt 2 tablespoons olive oil

Directions:

Pat dry zucchini slices and then spread them in an even layer on a baking sheet lined with parchment sheet. Whisk together salt and oil, brush this mixture over zucchini slices on both sides and then bake for 2 hours or more until brown and crispy. When done, let the chips cool for 10 minutes and then serve straight away.

Quinoa Broccoli Tots

Preparation time: 10 minutes Cooking time: 20 minutes Servings: 16

Ingredients:

2 tablespoons quinoa flour 2 cups steamed and chopped broccoli florets 1/2 cup nutritional yeast 1 teaspoon garlic powder 1 teaspoon miso paste 2 flax eggs 2 tablespoons hummus

Directions:

Place all the ingredients in a bowl, stir until well combined, and then shape the mixture into sixteen small balls. Arrange the balls on a baking sheet lined with parchment paper, spray with oil and bake at 400 degrees F for 20 minutes until brown, turning halfway. When done, let the tots cool for 10 minutes and then serve straight away

Nacho Kale Chips

Preparation time: 10 minutes Cooking time: 14 hours Servings: 10

Ingredients:

2 bunches of curly kale 2 cups cashews, soaked, drained 1/2 cup chopped red bell pepper 1 teaspoon garlic powder 1 teaspoon salt 2 tablespoons red chili powder 1/2 teaspoon smoked paprika 1/2 cup nutritional yeast 1 teaspoon cayenne 3 tablespoons lemon juice 3/4 cup water

Directions:

Place all the ingredients except for kale in a food processor and pulse for 2 minutes until smooth. Place kale in a large bowl, pour in the blended mixture, mix until coated, and dehydrate for 14 hours at 120 degrees F until crispy. If dehydrator is not available, spread kale between two baking sheets and bake for 90 minutes at 225 degrees F until crispy, flipping halfway. When done, let chips cool for 15 minutes and then serve.

Tomato Hummus

Preparation time: 5 minutes Cooking time: 0 minute Servings: 4

Ingredients:

1/4 cup sun-dried tomatoes, without oil 1 ½ cups cooked chickpeas 1 teaspoon minced garlic 1/2 teaspoon salt 2 tablespoons sesame oil 1 tablespoon lemon juice 1 tablespoon olive oil 1/4 cup of water

Directions:

Place all the ingredients in a food processor and process for 2 minutes until smooth. Tip the hummus in a bowl, drizzle with more oil, and then serve straight away.

Marinated Mushrooms

Preparation time: 10 minutes Cooking time: 7 minutes Servings: 6

Ingredients:

12 ounces small button mushrooms 1 teaspoon minced garlic 1/4 teaspoon dried thyme 1/2 teaspoon sea salt 1/2 teaspoon dried basil 1/2 teaspoon red pepper flakes 1/4 teaspoon dried oregano 1/2 teaspoon maple syrup 1/4 cup apple cider vinegar 1/4 cup and 1 teaspoon olive oil 2 tablespoons chopped parsley

Directions:

Take a skillet pan, place it over medium-high heat, add 1 teaspoon oil and when hot, add mushrooms and cook for 5 minutes until golden brown. Meanwhile, prepare the marinade and for this, place remaining ingredients in a bowl and whisk until combined. When mushrooms have cooked, transfer them into the bowl of marinade and toss until well coated. Serve straight away

Nacho Cheese Sauce

Preparation time: 5 minutes Cooking time: 10 minutes Servings: 4

Ingredients:

3 tablespoons flour 1/4 teaspoon garlic salt 1/4 teaspoon salt 1/2 teaspoon cumin 1/4 teaspoon paprika 1 teaspoon red chili powder 1/8 teaspoon cayenne powder 1 cup vegan cashew yogurt 1 1/4 cups vegetable broth

Directions:

Take a small saucepan, place it over medium heat, pour in vegetable broth, and bring it to a boil. Then whisk together flour and yogurt, add to the boiling broth, stir in all the spices, switch heat to medium-low level and cook for 5 minutes until thickened. Serve straight away.

Cinnamon Bananas

Preparation time: 5 minutes Cooking time: 8 minutes Servings: 2

Ingredients:

2 bananas, peeled, sliced 1 teaspoon cinnamon 2 tablespoons granulated Splenda 1/4 teaspoon nutmeg

Directions:

Prepare the cinnamon mixture and for this, place all the ingredients in a bowl, except for banana, and stir until mixed. Take a large skillet pan, place it over medium heat, spray with oil, add banana slices and sprinkle with half of the prepared cinnamon mixture. Cook for 3 minutes, then sprinkle with remaining prepared cinnamon mixture and continue cooking for 3 minutes until tender and hot. Serve straight away.

Pumpkin Cake Pops

Preparation time: 10 minutes Cooking time: 10 minutes Servings: 4

Ingredients:

1 cup coconut flour ¼ teaspoon cinnamon 1/4 cup coconut sugar 1/4 cup chocolate chips, unsweetened 3/4 cup pumpkin puree

Directions:

Place all the ingredients in a bowl, except for chocolate chips, stir until incorporated, and then fold in chocolate chips until combined. Shape the mixture into small balls, then place them on a cookie sheet greased with oil and bake for 10 minutes at 350 degrees F until done. Let the balls cool completely and then serve.

Turmeric Snack Bites

Preparation time: 35 minutes Cooking time: 0 minute
Servings: 10

Ingredients:

1 cup Medjool dates, pitted, chopped 1/2 cup walnuts 1 teaspoon ground turmeric 1 tablespoon cocoa powder, unsweetened 1/2 teaspoon ground cinnamon 1/2 cup shredded coconut, unsweetened

Directions:

Place all the ingredients in a food processor and pulse for 2 minutes until a smooth mixture comes together. Tip the mixture in a bowl and then shape it into ten small balls, 1 tablespoon of the mixture per ball and then refrigerate for 30 minutes. Serve straight away.

Lightning Source UK Ltd.
Milton Keynes UK
UKHW050226270521
384401UK00008B/77